Great African Americans

Mary McLeod Bethune

a great teacher

Revised Edition

Patricia and Fredrick McKissack

 Enslow Publishers, Inc.

40 Industrial Road	PO Box 38
Box 398	Aldershot
Berkeley Heights, NJ 07922	Hants GU12 6BP
USA	UK

http://www.enslow.com

To our friends Linda and Rob

Revised edition of *Mary McLeod Bethune: A Great Teacher* © 1991

Library of Congress Cataloging-in-Publication Data

McKissack, Pat, 1944–
    Mary McLeod Bethune: a great teacher / Patricia and Fredrick McKissack.— Rev. ed.
            p. cm. — (Great African Americans)
    Includes index.
        ISBN 0-7660-1680-3
    1. Bethune, Mary McLeod, 1875–1955—Juvenile literature. 2. African American women—Biography—Juvenile literature. 3. African American women educators—Biography—Juvenile literature. 4. African American women social reformers—Biography—Juvenile literature. 5. African Americans—Education—History—20th century—Juvenile literature. 6. African Americans—Civil rights—History—20th century—Juvenile literature. 7. United States—Race relations—Juvenile literature. [1. Bethune, Mary McLeod, 1875–1955. 2. Teachers. 3. African Americans—Biography. 4. Women—Biography.] I. McKissack, Fredrick. II. Title. III. Series.
    E185.97.B34 M37   2001
    370'.92—dc21
                                           00-012418

To Our Readers:
We have done our best to make sure all Internet addresses in this book were active and appropriate when we went to press. However, the author and the publisher have no control over and assume no liability for the material available on those Internet sites or on other Web sites they may link to. Any comments or suggestions can be sent by e-mail to comments@enslow.com or to the address on the back cover.

Every effort has been made to locate all copyright holders of material used in this book.
If any errors or omissions have occurred, corrections will be made in future editions of this book.

Illustration Credits: Bethune-Cookman College Office of Public Relations, pp. 7T, 15, 18, 20T, 20B. Courtesy Moody Bible Institute Archives, p. 10; Library of Congress, pp. 6, 14, 16, 19, 25T, 26, 27; Moorland-Spingarn Research Center, Howard University, pp. 3, 12, 13, 21, 23, 24, 25B; National Park Service–Mary McLeod Bethune Council House NHS, Washington, D.C., pp. 4, 7B, 9, 28.

Cover Illustration: Bethune-Cookman College Office of Public Relations; Courtesy Moody Bible Institute Archives; Library of Congress; Moorland-Spingarn Research Center, Howard University; National Park Service—Mary McLeod Bethune Council House NHS, Washington, D.C.

table of contents

1 I Will Read! 5

2 School Days 8

3 A Dream and $1.50 11

4 The Black Rose 17

5 From Cotton Fields
to the White House 22

Timeline 29

Words to Know................... 30

Learn More About
Mary McLeod Bethune 31
(Books and Internet Addresses)

Index.......................... 32

Mary McLeod Bethune
July 10, 1875–May 18, 1955

CHAPTER 1

I Will Read!

It was the summer of 1875. Patsy and Sam McLeod's (sounds like Mac-Loud) fifteenth child was born. Her name was Mary Jane McLeod.

It was a happy time for the family. Patsy and Sam had been slaves. Mary Jane was their first child born free! That made Mary Jane McLeod special.

Mary Jane grew up in a large and loving family in Mayesville, South Carolina. She rode

Picking cotton all day long is hard, hot work.

Old Bush, the family mule, to the fields. She picked cotton along with her brothers and sisters on her father's farm.

One day Mary Jane went with her mother to a large house. Her mother washed and ironed for the people who lived there. Mary Jane had never been in such a big house. A young girl who lived there showed Mary Jane around.

6

There was a book on a table. Mary Jane opened it. Suddenly the girl took it away, saying, "Put that book down! You can't read it anyway!"

Mary Jane was surprised and hurt. True, she couldn't read. But why did picking up a book make the other girl so angry?

The McLeods had a Bible. Nobody could read it. That night, Mary Jane held the book in her hand. "I will read!" she said. "God willing, I will read!"

Mary Jane's parents, Samuel and Patsy McLeod, above, were slaves until 1865. Mary was born in this log cabin, left.

CHAPTER 2

School Days

One day Miss Emma Wilson came to Mayesville. She told Sam and Patsy about the school she was starting. Would they send Mary Jane to school?

Sam didn't think so. He needed everybody to help in the fields. Mary Jane prayed softly. Patsy spoke to Sam alone. At last Sam gave in. Mary Jane could go to school.

Mary Jane's brothers and sisters were disappointed. Why couldn't she read after the first day in school? It took time. Before long Mary Jane did learn how to read and write. On one special night, she read the Bible to her mother and father. They were so proud.

Miss Wilson's school went to the sixth grade. A kind woman paid for Mary to go to the Scotia Seminary in Concord, North Carolina. In 1887 Mary went away to school.

"I will read!" said Mary as a young girl. She asked her parents to send her to school to learn.

She was just twelve years old. It was so lonely at first. She missed her family very much. Seven years later Mary finished Scotia. Then she went to Moody Bible College in Chicago. Mary Jane McLeod was ready to start her life's work. But what would it be? she wondered.

Mary and other Moody Bible students rode around Chicago in "gospel wagons." They visited people in hospitals and jails and taught Sunday school.

CHAPTER 3

A Dream and $1.50

mary wanted to teach in Africa. Instead she took a teaching job in Georgia. Good teachers were needed there.

Mary met Albertus Bethune. He was a teacher too. He made her laugh. They were happy together. In 1898 Mary and Albertus married. A year later, their son was born. His name was Albert McLeod Bethune. Everyone called him Bert.

Mrs. Bethune heard there was no school for

11

Mrs. Bethune could pick up the telephone and call very important people and ask for their help.

black children in Daytona Beach, Florida. Mrs. Bethune went there.

"I want to start a school for Negro girls," she said. All she had was $1.50. Some people laughed. Others helped.

Mrs. Bethune would not give up her dream. First she rented a small house. She found writing paper

12

**Mary's marriage to Albertus didn't last long.
She moved to Daytona Beach, Florida, with little Bert.**

Mrs. Bethune's school grew and grew. Here she is standing in front of White Hall with some of the students.

in the trash. She used boxes for desks and coal for pencils. It was a poor beginning.

But on October 3, 1904, Mrs. Bethune opened her school. She had five students. By 1905 the school had one hundred students and three teachers.

Next she bought land that had been the city trash dump. That is where she would build her school. Some people laughed. But others helped. Rich, important people gave money to help build her school . . . and a hospital, too.

The first building for the school was finished in 1906. It was called Faith Hall, because faith had built it.

In 1918 Mrs. Bethune, right, visited another school that had opened for black children in Florida.

**Mrs. Bethune's students called her
"Mother Dear" or "The Black Rose."**

CHAPTER 4

The Black Rose

n 1925 Mrs. Bethune's school joined with Cookman, an all-boys school. Bethune-Cookman became a grade school, high school, and college. Boys and girls went to school together.

Mrs. Bethune was the school's first president. But to her students, she was always just "Mother Dear."

Another name for Mrs. Bethune was "The Black Rose." This is how she got that name:

**Mrs. Bethune named her first school building
Faith Hall. After many years, her school joined with a boys'
school. She began teaching boys, too.**

Mrs. Bethune spoke all over the country. One idea she talked about was a big "people garden." She said that people are like flowers. They live together in the world just as flowers grow in a garden. Red, yellow, small, tall—all growing together. They are all different. But each one is lovely.

Once a child said to Mrs. Bethune that blacks couldn't live in the "people garden." There were no black flowers! This made Mrs. Bethune feel sad. "Just because you have not seen a thing doesn't mean it doesn't exist," she always said.

Many years later she got a wonderful surprise. While in the country of Holland, Mrs. Bethune was given the bulbs of black tulips, the first black flower.

Bert was Mrs. Bethune's only child. He was a teacher, too.

At Bethune-
Cookman
College,
students were
taught useful
skills like
cooking
and sewing
clothes.

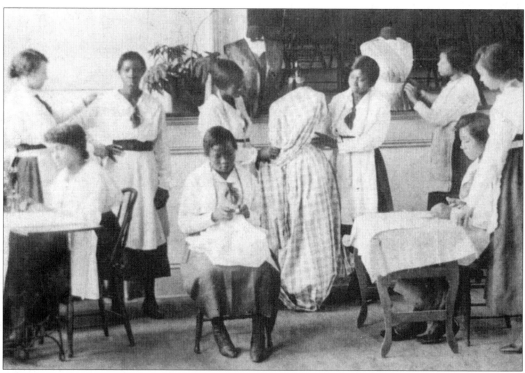

In Switzerland Mrs. Bethune was shown the black rose. This made her very happy. "Just because you have not seen a thing doesn't mean it doesn't exist."

She ordered seventy-two black rose bushes. They were planted at Bethune-Cookman College. She also had black tulips planted at the entrance of her school.

Mrs. Bethune was a well-known speaker. She spoke at churches and schools all over the coutry.

CHAPTER 5

From Cotton Fields to the White House

n 1932 Franklin D. Roosevelt was elected president of the United States. The president asked Mrs. Bethune to serve in the National Youth Administration (NYA). This organization helped people ages sixteen to twenty-four find part-time jobs. Mrs. Bethune was the first African-American woman to hold a job that high up in the government. It was an honor.

**The NAACP awarded Mrs. Bethune the Spingarn Medal in 1935.
At left is Mrs. Bethune's good friend Eleanor Roosevelt.**

Mrs. Bethune, right, protested for equal rights and fair treatment of African Americans.

Mrs. Eleanor Roosevelt was the president's wife. She was a friend to Mrs. Bethune. At the time, some people didn't think a black

"Help stop the murder!" Mrs. Bethune fought for laws to stop lynchings.

person should be invited to the White House. But the Roosevelts did. Mrs. Bethune was always welcome at the White House and in the Oval Office, too.

Mrs. Bethune worked for many different causes. Here she helps raise money for cancer research.

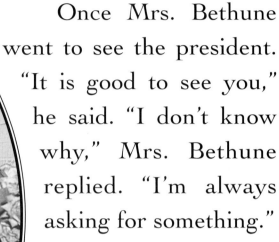

Many groups invited Mrs. Bethune to speak at special times. Here she gave a speech at a school graduation.

Once Mrs. Bethune went to see the president. "It is good to see you," he said. "I don't know why," Mrs. Bethune replied. "I'm always asking for something."

"Yes," said the president, "but you never ask for yourself."

It was true. Mrs. Bethune worked hard in the NYA. She tried to help young students find work so they could go to school. On April 25, 1945, Mrs. Bethune took part in the founding of the United Nations. Countries from all over the world agreed to work together for peace.

**Mrs. Bethune lived the last few years of her life at "The Retreat."
It was her home at Bethune-Cookman College.**

Mrs. Bethune lived the rest of her life at Bethune-Cookman College. There she died of a heart attack on May 18, 1955.

The school that Mary McLeod Bethune started with $1.50 is still in Daytona Beach. It helps prove that hard work can make dreams come true.

**Mrs. Bethune was the first African-American woman to head
a federal office, the National Youth Administration.
"I cannot rest while there is a single Negro boy or girl
lacking the chance to prove his worth," she said.**

Title:
Mary McLeod Bethune /
Item ID:
39549003974269
Call Number:
JB BETHUNE,M.
Out: 02/08/2018
5:23 PM
Due: 03/08/2018
11:59 PM
Renewals 1
Remaining

Title: Mixed me! /
Item ID:
39549005460747
Call Number JP DIG
Out: 02/08/2018
5:23 PM
Due: 03/08/2018
11:59 PM
Renewals 1
Remaining

Title:
How to play popular piano in
10 easy lessons /
Item ID:
39549003992444
Call Number: 786 2 MON
Out: 02/08/2018
5:23 PM
Due: 03/08/2018
11:59 PM
Renewals 1
Remaining

Current fine $0.00
balance

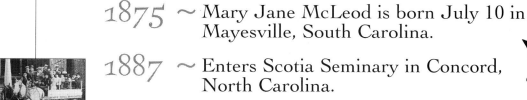

timeLiNe

1875 ~ Mary Jane McLeod is born July 10 in Mayesville, South Carolina.

1887 ~ Enters Scotia Seminary in Concord, North Carolina.

1894 ~ Enters Moody Bible College in Chicago.

1894

1898 ~ Begins to work as a teacher; marries Albertus Bethune.

1904 ~ Opens a school for African-American children in Daytona Beach, Florida.

1906 ~ Buys land for a bigger school and begins building it.

1925 ~ Bethune College joins with an all-boys school, Cookman College.

1932 ~ Serves in the National Youth Administration in Washington, D.C.

1935 ~ Receives the Spingarn Medal from the NAACP; founds the National Council of Negro Women.

1945 ~ Takes part in the founding of the United Nations.

1955 ~ Dies May 18 in Daytona Beach, Florida.

WORDS to KNOW

heart attack—An illness caused when a heart stops working properly. A person can die from a heart attack.

Moody Bible College—A college in Chicago started in 1886. It is now called the Moody Bible Institute.

National Association for the Advancement of Colored People (NAACP)—An organization started to help all Americans gain equal rights and protection under the law. The NAACP is one of the oldest civil rights organizations in the United States.

National Youth Administration (NYA)—An organization that helps young people.

Oval Office—The president's office. It is oval-shaped.

president—The leader of a country or group.

Scotia Seminary—An all-black school started in 1867 to teach former slaves and their children.

slave—A person who is owned by another. That person can be bought or sold.

United Nations—An organization of many countries who work together for peace.

White House—The house where the president of the United States lives.

Learn more about Mary McLeod Bethune

Books

Jones, Amy Robin. *Mary McLeod Bethune*. Chanhassen, Minn.: Child's World, Inc., 2000.

Greenfield, Eloise. *Mary McLeod Bethune*. New York, N.Y.: HarperCollins Children's Books, 1994.

McLoone, Margo. *Mary McLeod Bethune: A Photo-Illustrated Biography*. Mankato, Minn.: Bridgestone Books, 1997.

Internet Addresses

Mary McLeod Bethune Council House
Information about Mrs. Bethune, with photos.
<http://www.nps.gov/mamc/bethune/meet/main.htm>

Bethune-Cookman College
A short biography of Mrs. Bethune.
<http://www.cookman.edu/welcome/founder/founder.html>

National Woman's Hall of Fame
<http://www.greatwomen.org/profs/bethune_m.php>

index

a

Africa, 11

B

Bethune, Albert (Bert)
    McLeod (son), 11,
    13, 19
Bethune, Albertus
    (husband), 11, 13
Bethune-Cookman
    College, 14–18, 20,
    21, 27
    Faith Hall, 15, 18
    White Hall, 14
Bethune, Mary Jane
    McLeod
    and black flowers,
    19, 21
    as cotton picker,
    6
    birthplace, 7
    founding of her
    school, 12–15
    learning to read,
    7, 9
    marriage, 11, 13
    nicknames, 16,
    17–18

C

Chicago, Illinois, 10
Concord, North
    Carolina, 9

ð

Daytona Beach,
    Florida, 12, 13, 27

G

Georgia, 11

L

lynching, 25

m

Mayesville, South
    Carolina, 5, 8
McLeod Hospital, 15
McLeod, Patsy
    (mother), 5, 6,
    7, 8
McLeod, Sam (father),
    5, 7, 8
Moody Bible College,
    10

N

National Association for
    the Advancement of
    Colored People
    (NAACP), 23
National Youth
    Administration
    (NYA), 22, 26, 28

O

Old Bush, 6

R

Retreat, The, 27
Roosevelt, Eleanor, 23,
    25
Roosevelt, Franklin D.,
    22, 25, 26

S

Scotia Seminary, 9, 10
Spingarn Medal, 23

U

United Nations, 26

W

White House, 25
    Oval Office, 25
Wilson, Miss Emma, 8